TIME MANAGEMENT
MANIFESTO

Expert Strategies to Create an Effective Work/Life Balance

BY THOMAS B. DOWD III

This book is dedicated to the person who didn't have time to read it, but found that time anyway. You're about to do more personally and professionally than you ever dreamed.

Time Management Manifesto
© 2014 by Thomas B. Dowd III

All rights reserved.

Printed in the United States of America.

No part of this book may be used or reproduced in any manner whatsoever without written permission except in the case of brief quotations embodied in critical articles and reviews.

This publication is designed to provide information in regard to the subject matter covered. In so doing, neither the publisher nor the author is engaged in rendering legal, accounting or other professional services. If you require legal advice or other expert assistance, you should seek the services of a professional specializing in the particular discipline required.

While the author has made every effort to provide accurate information at the time of publication, neither the publisher nor the author assumes any responsibility for errors, or for changes that occur after publication.

First Edition

Cover & Book Design: Nu-Image Design
ISBN: 978-1503017474

Note: The views expressed are my own and not those of my current or former employers.

—Thomas B. Dowd III

Praise for *Time Management Manifesto*

"Wow! This powerful, practical book shows you how to get your time and your life under control—immediately."

    - Brian Tracy, author of *Ultimate Sales Success*

"As I balance the time crunches of having different hats including husband, father, radio host and football analyst, I know the constant effort needed to balance work and life. *Time Management Manifesto* is an effective and easily digestible book to remind readers that it can all be done well."

    - Rich Gannon, 17-year NFL QB, 4-time Pro Bowler,
      NFL MVP, Sirius NFL Radio & CBS NFL Analyst

"The *Time Management Manifesto* is a breath of fresh air. I love the way it says in the introduction that it contains no secrets. Rather, it is brimming with sound, practical advice. Its brilliance is also in its brevity. So many personal and business development books these days are bigger than they need to be. This book contains 30 wonderful time management nuggets. Read just one a day for a month and your relationship with time will change forever. Although, you can read the book in next to no time, it is a book that you will want to dip into time and time again."

    - Tom Evans, author of *The Zone* and creator of *Living Timefully*

"As an author and self-proclaimed student of inspiration, I've been inspired by many great motivational authors over the years. When it comes to the subject of time management, Tom Dowd's book *Time Management Manifesto* is among the best. *Time Management Manifesto* delivers and inspires, and in my mind this book puts Tom in the class with the great Stephen R. Covey."

    - Dominick Domasky, Motivational Speaker,
      author of *Don't Double Bread the Fish*

"*Time Management Manifesto* is a must for the busy professional. Though my family would say otherwise, I've always fancied myself as someone who is effective and efficient at scheduling time and activities. But as I read the *Manifesto*, I saw glaring grievances of how I'm actually wasting productivity in my day. I now admit it…I've been an email junkie! We all get out of sync sometimes and *Time Management Manifesto* helps to put our priorities back in proper perspective."

    - Doreen Lecheler, Transformational Thought Leader, Best-Selling author, *The Mind to Heal*

"Very few situations in life flare up the stress hormones in the body more than too much to do and too little time to do it all. To manage your time successfully is an art that requires a 'how-to' skill set. Tom Dowd offers readers practical how-to solutions to accomplish an innate desire of any working professional: do more in less time, without all of the stress. This is a powerful read to help you work less and have more."

    - Lauren Miller, Author/Speaker/Founder of StressSolutionsUniversity.com, LaurenEMiller.com

"I found the book to be very wise, practical, beautifully prioritized, and honest! The most precious of all moments is NOW. In *Time Management Manifesto: Expert Strategies to Create an Effective Work/Life Balance*, Tom Dowd offers a tremendously practical and simple formula to get off of the endless and empty road called 'as soon as' and truly make the most of the now. In today's technologically accelerating world, simple is genius. Dowd helps us create momentum in our lives with simple, clear principles that will make your days richer, fuller, and more balanced."

    - Brian Biro, "America's Breakthrough Coach"

"Tom Dowd effectively describes how time management skills can be developed as a way of being kinder, gentler, and more honest with oneself. By being self-aware, a person becomes more powerful, and *Time Management Manifesto: Expert Strategies to Create an Effective Work/Life Balance* is all about consciously behaving in ways that put you first while also improving your relationships and avoiding stress, shame, and guilt."

- Heather Hans, LCSW, MSW, MBA, CPIC,
author of *The Heart of Self-Love: How to Radiate with Confidence*

"These are practical tips for today's fast-paced world. Just a title of any tip, like 'Blending Work and Life Schedules' gives a hint maybe your daily schedule is in need of a tune-up. The book is solid in tried-and-true time management principles and relevant to today. Dowd's book is an asset to help get better charge of your time, and get an energy boost in the process."

- Patricia Weber, author of *Communication Toolkit for Introverts*

"Tom Dowd's *Time Management Manifesto* grabbed my attention from the beginning because of Tom's down-to-earth style, honesty, and stories that bring each point home. As someone who has facilitated and attended many time management programs, I found one key thing that makes Tom's book stand out from the rest—it was balance. Many books and programs can help you cram more work into your day. However, Tom's approach is to help the reader create a balanced life; the only way to achieve true productivity. Tom not only teaches the practical elements of time management, but helps the reader truly understand each concept by presenting the psychology behind it. A must-read for professionals seeking to achieve real work-life balance."

- Amy Castro, speaker, trainer, and author of
*Practical Communication: 25 Tips, Tools,
and Techniques for Getting Along and Getting Things Done*

"Tom's latest book on how valuable and precious our time actually is to us is spot on! Successful people are the masters of their time and are exceptional time managers... always."

- Don Holbrook, author of *The Next America 2nd Edition*

"In this age where all of us are bombarded with 'too much information' Tom Dowd reminds us there is hope. This practical and doable guide gives us the opportunity to create our own processes to manage the barrage. His tips are incredibly useful and applicable immediately. I highly recommend this important manifesto to help achieve success both at work and at home."

- Wally Hauck, PhD, author of *Stop the Leadership Malpractice: How to Replace the Typical Performance Appraisal*

"This *Manifesto* is perfect for the busy professional, the busy mom and for anyone who struggles to keep their day on track. I loved the emphasis on being realistic when setting deadlines, as too many of us tend to underestimate the time needed when we are striving to be the top performer in the boss's eyes. We end up sabotaging our own efforts!"

- Nancy Powell Bartlett, author of *The 180 Rule for Accountability*

"Tom's book *Time Management Manifesto: Expert Strategies to Create an Effective Work/Life Balance* manages the balance of easy-to-read and effective teaching tips with an effective simplicity. Time spent learning from Tom will make you more efficient and stress-free immediately.

- Lynette Louise, The Brain Broad! Internationally renowned author, composer, radio and TV host, brain therapist for intentional change

"Tom summarizes the key to time management as, 'Time Management is a disciplined mindset to be able to live in the moment while working toward the future.' He then describes how to apply this philosophy to our own work and personal lives. Even at 80 years of age, I find his suggestions pertinent and extremely helpful."

- Jim R. Olson, author of *4 Star Retirement-2 Star Budget*

"Tom's book fascinated me from the very start through to the very end. It was full of captivating lessons, directly applicable to my life as a trainer and public speaker. There are two powerful statements that resonated in my mind after reading the book, 'I own my twenty-four hours each day—I don't rent them,' and, 'If you can't manage your time well, you'll be playing catch with one of your kids one day and your mind will be elsewhere trying to remember what you need to do next.'"

- Vaida Bogdan, Experiential Trainer in Time Management and Personality Typologies

"Tom has done everyone who doesn't have enough time in their day a big favor with *Time Management Manifesto*. Wonderfully short, this little book is packed with great practical tips for maximizing the 24 hours everyone does have."

- Kita Szpak, Happiness Expert and Speaker, author of *The SIMPLE Life: Shiny Objects Not Required*

"Tom Dowd's book has many great strategies and ideas. The common thread is 'Take Control!' We have the power and it is up to each of us to make it happen. Thanks for the reminder, Tom."

- Julie Ann Sullivan, The Attitude Enhancer

"Timeless wisdom for the professional who desires to enjoy the time of their life. Tom packs actionable productivity tips into this must-read book."

- Jeff Krantz, author of *Sales ROCKSTAR: How Top Producers Perform,* and multi-award winning sales trainer

Contents

Introduction 1

Balancing Professional and Personal Time 4

Making People a Priority 6

Building Time for the Unexpected 8

Doing the Least Amount of Work in a Day 11

Using Recurring Appointments 13

Sleeping Better 15

Being Realistic with Deadlines 16

Accounting for Ancillary Time 18

Following Up 20

Learning to Touch it Once 22

Investing Time to Save Time 24

Getting Things Done with Teammates 26

Assessing Your Checklist Habits 28

Creating Effective Checklists 31

Monitoring Multitasking 33

Committing Yourself 35

Taking Time to Assess Strategies 37

Managing Your Email 40

Setting the Alarm 43

Blending Work and Life Schedules 45

Being Curious 47

Understanding Priorities 49

Accounting for Personal Conversations 51

Creating Our Own Pressures 53

Taking Notes 55

Putting Off Tasks 57

Making Decisions 59

Asking for Help 61

Creating Time for You 63

Taking Back Your Day 65

References 67

Acknowledgements 69

Also by Thomas B. Dowd III 71

About the Author 74

INTRODUCTION

The first time I can remember being called *anal retentive,* I debated whether it was a good thing or a bad thing. According to Memidex/WordNet Dictionary/Thesaurus, it is a person, "who pays such attention to detail that the obsession becomes an annoyance to others, potentially to the detriment of the anal-retentive person. The term derives from Freudian psychoanalysis." I guess a description using words like psychoanalysis and obsession can't always be seen as good, but the term grew on me. The reference to anal retentive was typically about making sure things got done. Nowhere in the description does it mention the words time, organization, or time management. Yet, when people say they *don't have time*, they are really saying they didn't get done everything they wanted to get done. Now is the time to do *everything* you want to do. This book may not create obsessive anal-retentive monsters, but it will create methodologies to help you pay attention to the right priorities.

Even at work when I was riding a rollercoaster of success that included some interesting curves and downhill dives, I made the effort to constantly hone my time management and organizational skills to not only keep my nose above water, but to prove people wrong. When I was demoted twice for being in the right place at the wrong time—not being mature enough yet to manage the efforts of people—nobody could say it wasn't because the work wasn't getting done. I ironically found the maturity by sharing all of my mistakes with others!

I've taught versions of the time management information included in this book for more than fifteen years. There are four points I want to emphasize. First, the word secret is nowhere to be found in this book.

- There are no secrets to time management. Commitment, routine, and a number of other factors will make you successful, but there is no secret formula to time management. As you find the balance that works for you, you will find success.

- Second, as attached as we may be to the latest and greatest technology gadgets and applications that claim to make us more efficient, they are only supporting tools to the process of time management. In fact, many of them—including social media—eat up large chunks of time before we even realize it. Your ability to execute what you set out to do will not be magically solved with a new smart phone.

- Third, your personal and professional lives are intertwined. You may not think that you take your work home with you. You may not even discuss it when you get home. However, you do think about it. *What do I have to do tomorrow? Was I supposed to send that email? Did I ever get back to my boss?* A dozen random thoughts from your professional world worm their way into the sanctity of your home life, regardless of how much you try to keep them separate.

- Finally, for as long as I've shared my time management tips, it has been rare that I've made significant changes to what I'm teaching. It's not because I haven't evolved with time. I've found that people overcomplicate the process, or find excuses as opposed to solutions. Let's oversimplify, instead, with *Time Management Manifesto.*

I sleep very well. Most nights, I sleep more than the recommended eight hours. I am refreshed and ready for each day. I balance my full-time job with my other business, while still making it to my children's piano recitals, field hockey games, school events, and so much more. I mention this not to say, 'look how much I can jam into a day.' I truly don't feel like I jam anything into my days. I simply prepare for all of them ahead of time. I own my twenty-four hours each day—I don't rent them. It's up to me to determine how they are used. I'm accountable. I must make decisions each day based on my priorities and account for unexpected time by thinking forward and being flexible. If there is such thing as a traditional forty-hour work week, I'm confident enough to be able to say that I do more in it than most people do in fifty, sixty, and even seventy hours. It's *time* to work smarter—not harder—and start taking back the twenty-four hours in *your* day to actually get *more* done personally and professionally.

BALANCING PROFESSIONAL AND PERSONAL TIME

I was sitting in a company-sponsored time management class as a new manager at the ripe age of twenty-four. I held in my hand my brand new time management binder that, I was sure, would solve all my problems. The instructor made a comment that has unintentionally stuck with me for years: "If you can't manage your time well, you'll be playing catch with one of your kids one day and your mind will be elsewhere, trying to remember what you need to do next." Fast forward to many years later, when I was kicking a soccer ball around in the yard with my oldest when I found my mind wandering. I was distracted with work thoughts. My personal and professional lives were bleeding together.

Welcome to the modern world, where there is inevitably a blur between work and home. Yet, we have control over more than we think. The boss may be barking instructions, your email inbox is blowing up, and you have to post that picture of what you ate last night on Facebook. It can all be done. Time management isn't about a new binder or even an electronic device. It is a disciplined mindset that allows you to live in the moment while working toward the future. Time management is often a mental game—but the concept of time management doesn't have to be hard. It's about commitment, routines, flexibility, adjustments, and planning. We create our own self-limitations. We say we'll do tomorrow what we really want to do today. You must eliminate what's holding you back.

You can't come home after a day of work and completely clear your head—can you? Yes. It starts with taking inventory. I don't want you to start a time study. They are too subjective, the data sources too unreliable. Instead, I want you to write down the top three things that take up most of your time at work, regardless of whether they're required or not. Think it through. Not what took your time yesterday; think about what consistently occupies your day. The goal of this book is to gain efficiency where and when you can, even if it takes small steps. By keeping it top of mind as you continue to read through *Time Management Manifesto*, you'll start to adapt your most time-consuming methods and habits to find the balance you've always wanted.

Time management is a requirement for all people in all roles—not just CEOs, managers, owners, or even individual contributors. If you think you don't have enough time to invest in order to improve your own time management, think again. There are only twenty-four hours in the day. They should not all be devoted to work, but if you don't manage the work piece, you can't balance the personal piece. Start immediately. Manage your time, don't let it manage you.

MAKING PEOPLE A PRIORITY

I was running to what I thought to be the most important meeting I ever had—I say with sarcasm. I mock myself because I can't even remember what the meeting was about. What I can remember is that someone who worked for me stopped me at my office door and asked for a couple of minutes of my time. I asked if it was important. The words said, "No;" the eyes that I remember so clearly said, "Definitely." I never saw her again. I found out later that she was having stress-related mental health issues. I could have easily found her the support and assistance she needed with a quick phone call. Instead, my schedule dictated where I needed to be and at what time.

Regardless of your schedule, people are the highest priority. When we die, our inbox will most likely not be empty. As we go through this book on time management, it's critical to understand that "how" you manage your time can influence others. It's also important to realize just how important people are. The ones we often complain about who are occupying our time, can actually make us all more productive if they feel like they are part of the solution, part of the team, and active members in supporting all of our time management challenges. All the while, these individuals teach us to make better judgments and assessments that will pay off later. This comes by building trust, respect, and support for the people who surround us personally and professionally. We can't do most things on our own.

Let's take the time to acknowledge that the clock may dictate where we should be and at what time, but we must also have a willingness to drop everything to take care of the matters that need our attention the most. This usually revolves around people! You must take action to ensure that you pay attention not just to words, but to the cues that people are sending with their body language.

When I teach this portion of my seminars, I'm often asked how this idea of making time for those around us can positively impact effective time management. After all, dealing with people not only takes up a lot of time, but it often takes time away from what needs to be accomplished. Besides the lesson I learned in the story about it simply being the right thing to do, this also pays off in the long run, because people see what you're willing to do for them. They, in turn, are more willing to reciprocate if you are ever in need. Not everything has to be burning with urgency, but you will find that time management is about working together with colleagues, co-workers, clients, and business partners so that everyone wins. Additionally, as your ability to assess what is really important and urgent becomes better, your ability to effectively prioritize will likewise improve.

BUILDING TIME FOR THE UNEXPECTED

Have you ever been deep in thought or just hit your stride on a project only to have it snatched away with a phone call, an incoming email that you caught from the corner of your eye, or worse, a loud ding from a device you're working with? Research has proven that it will take you up to seven times longer to come up with the thought you just had than it took for the original idea.

You must build in time for the unexpected—or as the business world affectionately calls them, fire drills. In an article entitled "Don't Let Technology Take Over," Dave Beck references a Basex study of over one-thousand office workers showing that interruptions consume more than two hours, or twenty-eight percent of a typical workday. To quote the article,

"More than half of those surveyed said they open email immediately or soon after it arrives, no matter how busy they are. The two hours of lost productivity included not only unimportant interruptions and distractions…but also the recovery time needed to get back on task. The study found that based on an average salary of $21 per hour for 'knowledge workers' whose jobs involve information, workplace interruptions cost the U.S. economy $588 billion a year."

Have you accounted for these two hours in your calendar? Have you trained yourself to jump in to actually deal with these interruptions?

Think about how you schedule your day. If you schedule all eight hours in a work day, you are guaranteed to not meet everything that's on your calendar. Look at your schedule for the coming week and start to block off time to account for fire drills—the things you didn't plan on dealing with today, but have no choice. Maybe the few minutes here and there don't need to make your calendar to deal with those small tasks, but you may need to account for it in other administrative or work action time. For example, if it takes you *thirty minutes* to typically do paperwork daily, schedule *an hour* for administrative purposes. Next, it's time to schedule specific time for real-work action like responding to emails and returning messages. Personally, I prefer the quiet morning time for email and later in the morning for phone calls, when possible. Next, identify other x-factors such as busier days of the week or seasonality, and make the adjustments. As another example, when I was a manager in a call center, we knew the call volume was heaviest on Mondays, so we built time for managers to be on the floor with the people on the phones that day, and made a point not to schedule Monday staff meetings.

You may be asking yourself, "Why does scheduling stuff I know I need to do each day need to make my calendar?" You probably already know that if you don't schedule it, it may not get done. Having the actual reminder will prompt you to get to it. These scheduled periods of time become a barrier of protection to show you what's *supposed to* be done today. The phrase *supposed to* is italicized because we know that planning a day doesn't always mean that's how the day will play out. By scheduling administrative work and overestimating the expected time, you are leaving a fire drill cushion.

You can't control all the interruptions that may come your way, but you can control your reaction to them. You don't want to be a slave to your calendar, but you do want to be committed to it when you can. Let's go back to the paperwork example. If you actually completed it in the expected time of thirty minutes and had no interruptions, you bought yourself some extra time to *pull* future work in from other days. If you did have some fire drills to deal with, you accounted for much of this with the reserved blocks of time.

DOING THE LEAST AMOUNT OF WORK IN A DAY

I was once in the middle of transitioning roles, so I met with the person whose job I would be taking over. I asked for a task list so I could get started. He handed me two. The first was a short list; the other was a much longer list, which included all the items from the first as well as several others. I asked him about the difference. He said the short list was the least amount of work he could do in a day and walk out of the office satisfied knowing that all critical items had been met. Since that day, I've managed around the concept of the "least amount of work I can do in a day."

You see, many of us think in terms of the longer list, creating high levels of stress when we don't accomplish everything. We, in turn, push our work from day to day like we used to push our vegetables on our plates as kids. We push it around but does it ever get consumed—or in this case, done?

Create your must-do short list, including what must be done during the day, the week, and the month. What is the least amount of work that can be done with you walking out satisfied that the job was done? The list can be ever evolving and reviewed regularly to ensure it remains updated. As you continue to massage the short checklist, you should block off the time to do each item by using your calendar as a tool to reserve time for this must-do list. Even if you don't have a designated time for these tasks, block off the amount of time anyway, as a way of acknowledging that they must be done at some point in the day.

For example, you know you need to do an hour of project work over several days. You may schedule it for two hours from ten a.m. to noon, but you can build in the flexibility to move this block of time through the day if something else comes up. Yes, I doubled the time, because if you don't do it today, the work still needs to be done and you've just pushed twice as much work to tomorrow. I recommend that you double all the time you expect things to take. The concept of doubling time is important. If you want to think you need thirty minutes to meet with someone, set the actual appointment for sixty minutes. As stated in the last chapter, expect the unexpected.

Instead of pushing tasks day to day—which actually takes time— start to use the extra time that you build into your calendar to *pull in* tasks from future days, weeks, and even months out. You must understand that consistently *pushing* to another day is a red flag. When you can account for the least amount of work that you can do in a day and consider yourself successful, you will walk away satisfied and benefit greatly from the power of the pull versus the push.

USING RECURRING APPOINTMENTS

I come into work each day and the first thing I do is read a passage from the most impactful book I ever read: Don't Sweat the Small Stuff, by Dr. Richard Carlson. Why? In addition to doing it as an inspiration boost each day, I do it because my calendar tells me to do it. It's been on my calendar for over ten years, and it pops up every morning at seven a.m. Naturally after all these years, I barely see it, because it's so ingrained to do it—but it gets done. I'm not curing the world of its ills with this task, but it shows that building the right habits will lead to stronger time management. More importantly, it's a great lesson: You don't have to think about what has to be done next if your calendar can do it for you. My calendar is filled with what many would consider silly reminders—but I also have far less stress because I know what's coming. Without even thinking, I get gently reminded to transition work and tasks.

Create your own recurring appointments. Invest time today to study your schedule and start to add basic appointments immediately. You can start with the ones that should be on everyone's calendar, regardless of position or role in an organization; the tasks that have nothing to do with your actual job responsibilities. First, add a five-minute appointment at the end of each work day to review and organize tomorrow. Actually schedule this event at the end of the day on the calendar. I promise you that you will sleep better knowing exactly what's on your plate for the next day. Five invested minutes will save you hours later!

Next, add an appointment to organize the following week each Friday—project out a week at a time and actually schedule this event on your calendar. Do the same thing at the end of each month based on regular monthly tasks, such as budgeting, for example. It's important to also be smart about *when* you do this. When I say end of the month, I'm not talking about the thirtieth. I'm actually thinking sometime around the twenty-sixth, so day one isn't sprung on you. This allows you to better spread out the tasks over the course of a month versus cramming everything into marathon sessions. Many of us like to procrastinate until the actual need to do something. Therefore, if you have multiple tasks that are due at the end of the month, you may not worry about them until the end of the month. Suddenly, a flood of pressure is on you to beat the impending deadline. Be someone who does not procrastinate until the end of the month—spread your tasks out during the month. The amount of time to complete these tasks throughout the month is the same time it will take to finish at the end of a month. The only difference is the amount of pressure you feel—and, most likely, the quality of work performed!

By creating recurring appointments, you're shifting much of the self-created pressures away from you to the calendar, and investing time to save time. You're now using your calendar as a tool to benefit you.

SLEEPING BETTER

I used to lie in bed and roll around with constant thoughts in my head: What do I have to do tomorrow? On no! Look at the clock. Tomorrow is now today. I would get ideas in my head, and keep kicking those ideas around to enable myself to remember them in the morning, thus sleeping poorly and often not even remembering it anyway. One of the greatest time management tips I can offer is a simple pad of paper at your nightstand. I'm now in the habit of waking up when I have an idea—most times I'm groggy, but it's now ingrained in me to immediately write it down. I then drift off for the best night sleep ever, knowing that my ideas or follow-up items are waiting for me when I wake up for the new day.

Grab a pad of paper and a pen, put it next to your nightstand, and simply wait for the ideas to flow. When random thoughts wake you, write them down immediately. This has numerous benefits. First, you won't forget. Second, you'll sleep better. Finally—and the greatest benefit of all—you will have stronger ideas since you have reached the inner non-stressed part of your brain.

BEING REALISTIC WITH DEADLINES

Are you the eager employee who volunteers for everything that comes your way in an attempt to advance within your organization? What is your confidence level when your boss or your boss's boss gives you an assignment when your plate is full? I remember working for an individual who was driving me hard. I made every effort to keep my tasks organized, so I maintained a spreadsheet. I had a column that noted all of my deadlines. Some were manager-assigned, while many were self-initiated, aggressive dates to work toward. I wanted to do everything possible to push myself and prove my worth. One day, I was providing an update to my manager, so I showed him the spreadsheet. Although thirty-seven of the forty items were on pace to be achieved on time, he focused on the three that were past due. The three that were past due were my own deadlines missed. Unfortunately, he held them over my head for quite some time.

I learned a valuable lesson that day: We must be realistic with our timeframes, regardless of how badly we want to meet them. We should continue to drive our work and not *sandbag* our deliverables, but we must balance it with everything we're doing. In our efforts to be "go-getters," we may actually be casting a negative shadow if we don't accomplish everything we said we would by the given timeframes.

Think back to the times when you were a go-getter and found some commitments not being fulfilled. Effective immediately, I want you to begin to under-promise and over-deliver. You shouldn't tell the boss that it will be done by five o'clock p.m. because you *hope* it will be done. You should tell the boss when you know it will be done. If five p.m. isn't the right timing, you should be honest and tell the boss when the realistic right time is, or invest time to reprioritize other tasks. If you haven't established a strong enough relationship to do this, you may want to begin to build the trust and respect required to have those prioritization discussions. By under-promising and over-delivering, you'll start to find appropriate times to hand work in early, beat deadlines, and often times start taking on more responsibilities. It's ironic how easy it is to stop being a go-getter and actually go out and get more done when you are real with your deadlines.

ACCOUNTING FOR ANCILLARY TIME

When I managed people in a call center, I used to like walking the floor at least once in the morning and once before I left for the day in order to talk with the employees. I often wondered where the time went in the day, and why there were times when I wasn't getting everything done I wanted to. I knew the people doing the hard work deserved my time, but I didn't know how I could continue to balance it. My peers were getting feedback that their employees never saw them, so I knew I was doing the right thing, but I didn't want my other work to suffer.

Then, I thought back to my own advice about blocking off time on the calendar. It was a lesson I'd been trying to teach others, and yet had completely missed the fact that it was the solution to my own problem! Although I could typically walk the floor in fifteen minutes, it wasn't on my calendar. I instantly scheduled thirty minutes to start the day and thirty minutes to finish the day, for walking the floor. I built in double the time to allow for extended conversations, problem solving, or getting caught in the hall with someone who wanted to share a lengthy story. As I started to figure out actual timing, I adjusted it down and input a middle-of-the-day walk, too. I was actually more efficient because I knew a calendar reminder would pop up—and over time, I knew it was coming and became better able to focus on my current tasks and meet all of my goals.

Do you account for everything you do in a day? Take the time to list out ancillary pieces that you may not have typically added to your calendar and add them. Some examples may include:

- Walking around/time not at your desk (e.g., water cooler or even a restroom break)
- Running into people in the hall/casual conversations with peers

Although you may not *schedule* these events, they *do* take your time. These previously unscheduled items can now be add-ons to the previously noted administrative block of time we discussed earlier. Have you accounted for this time? Using the blanket blocking of the time will allow you to know that time is still being taken up.

All of the efforts to account for time are about knowing what is taking up your time each day. That knowledge is a powerful thing, because it will ease the pressure you feel on yourself; if it's not done, it's not the end of the world. However, as you become more productive, you'll start to see more wins and sustained efficiency. In addition, on many calendar applications—Microsoft Outlook, Instant Messenger, and Skype, for example—those blocks of time you've set aside will show your peers that you are "busy," thus keeping requests for your time in check.

FOLLOWING UP

As I continued to come up the ranks as a new manager, I constantly heard focus group feedback about how lack of follow-through by leaders and managers was a key point of frustration for teams of employees. Whether it was to solve a problem, answer a question, or do some customer research, it didn't matter—the same managers' names came up time and time again. They were building a reputation—and not a good one.

Communication and follow-up are extremely important. Your ability to follow up with employees, clients, or peers is one of the clearest indications of the effectiveness of your organizational skills. When people are continually apprised of your progress, assumptions disappear and stress is greatly reduced. Even if deadlines must be extended or your progress isn't as far along as you'd hoped, your ability to communicate that clearly to all parties builds trust in the fact that movement is taking place.

Your online calendar should be a haven for follow-up appointments. As soon as you ask someone for something or they ask you for something by a certain date, your next inclination should be to immediately add it to your calendar. Then, the pressure is off of you to remember. Once you do this a few times, it will become second nature. Specific examples include calls to return or email responses. For email requests, many online calendars allow you to embed the actual email request into the calendar appointment itself. Now you're beginning to manage your inbox volume.

An important point to consider is to schedule these follow-up deadlines and appointments before they are due. If you owe your manager a presentation by five o'clock p.m. on Thursday, the appointment should not be seen for the first time at five o'clock on Thursday. You can use pop-up reminders or audible cues (alarms) if you are using an online calendar tool to your advantage. If you're still using a written calendar, you can use color coding or symbols to address urgency or action needed.

Your calendar is an important proactive tool to manage your follow-up items—not just the due dates, but the actual time to work on them and provide periodic updates to the person making the request. Be the leader who gets things done. Build the confidence of your peers, colleagues, direct reports, clients, and business partners, and never have their confidence in your ability to effectively follow up questioned.

LEARNING TO TOUCH IT ONCE

I would like to expand on the comment made in the previous chapter about managing your email inbox. I used to have a position as business support manager for a large operation. I was privy to my manager's inbox and was asked to periodically manage it for him. I thought it was an easy enough task—until the first time I saw his inbox and realized there were over one-thousand emails. Many were read, while many others were not. Some were important, others were not. Some were critical, with deadlines that had passed. I had some work to do. The most critical point when dealing with email is to touch it once. As soon as you've chosen to allow yourself to read it or even preview it, you must now do something with it. Leaving it in your inbox should not be an option. Learn to touch it once.

You can effectively manage your inbox with a few easy tips. I normally filter my inbox by time with the most recent on top. However, for this exercise, start by filtering your inbox by "Subject" and keep only the most recent one if it's a duplicate. Next, review for topics, subjects, or senders that come on a regular basis that you don't ever read. If you can or want to, click on unsubscribe. If you feel there may be a need to reference it in the future but don't read it often, establish a setting to send it directly to your trash, but know that you can get to it if you need to. Next, go through your current inbox and determine which emails have tasks or follow-up required. Make actual dates to work on them. Make appointments for following through by embedding or inserting the email into the calendar appointment. Email platforms with synchronized calendars will have tutorials or help if you need further details.

Read your emails once. Even if the email catches my eye as a preview, I have a rule of thumb to deal with it as soon as it's seen. It already distracted me, so I should put it in its proper place. We only have a few choices in how to handle it: delete it, save it to another file for future reference, move it to an appointment to do something about it later, or address it now. Touch it once.

INVESTING TIME TO SAVE TIME

Investing time to do something ahead of time saves time. Few people invest the time to read all their emails all the way through. For the most part, I am one of the few. I'm often asked how I manage my time effectively. One critical way is that I don't skim email—there's too much risk of missing critical information or creating more work by asking questions that are answered within the text. I read them start to finish, including the attachments. The easy argument for why not to do this is information overload, or that we don't have time. I agree. However, taken in the context of the touch-it-once principle I cited in the last chapter, this becomes more manageable.

I've learned that by staying ahead of my emails, I garner incremental time to invest in other places. I also avoid wasted time digging for answers on my own, because I know where and who to go to for information. If you don't know, invest time to learn. It saves time when you know the go-to contacts to fix certain problems. Additionally, you aren't wasting time asking people to resend information or asking questions that are answered later in the email that you chose not to read thoroughly.

Effective immediately, be the person who reads one-hundred percent of your emails from top to bottom, and invests time to read the attachments. There are often pre-determined assumptions that an email isn't relevant, or even portions of an email aren't relevant. However, reading it will allow you to make your own determination. If you find a pattern, you can decide to stop getting them or have a conversation with the senders about their messaging so it saves both of you time. Remember, you are attaining a competitive edge by gaining knowledge, while saving time because you may be becoming the subject-matter expert.

Next, you should schedule an hour once a week to learn another piece of your own business, take an online class, or meet with someone in another line of business. Another option is for you to dedicate this time to reading interesting articles or less urgent inbox items that come in during the week. You can insert the article right into the appointment for that dedicated time. This is your chance to be curious, learn from peers, and get lingering questions answered—all while saving future time.

When you become the go-to person and have the answers, you actually save time. We say we don't have time. What we're really saying is we're not willing to find the time, to invest the time, to actually save time.

GETTING THINGS DONE WITH TEAMMATES

To use a sports analogy, if you run with a ball on your own from point A to point B, it will take you longer than simply kicking it or throwing it to another person already at point B. We try to do too much on our own. Whether we want all the glory, think we can do it better, or simply just want it done, there is value in getting others involved. This chapter isn't about dumping, or even delegating. It's about teamwork. Depending on your position, you may still have to supervise, validate the work, or make sure it gets done, but you should find opportunities to avoid doing everything on your own.

Think about the expertise you have surrounding you. Do you have the right people working on the right tasks? Start to keep a list of contacts with their specific expertise so that you can quickly reference it. If you are part of a team effort, schedule time with your peers or co-workers, particularly if you're all depending on each other's contributions. The benefit of a routine get-together is that it allows people to obtain consolidated information in one sitting as opposed to communications going back and forth with "reply all" emails that can take up valuable time.

It's important to have a meaningful and added-value manner for people to get updates. If it's not a meeting, at least create a consistent time each week for a progress summary with everyone's contributions. The goal is to create a routine in which people know when and where updates and answers will be given, which reduces surprises and questions like, "Where do we stand on project A?" If you do set up a progress report email, be sensitive to the amount of time it's taking everyone. You want meaningful content, but not time wasted for emails that go unread or administrative tasks that take away from actually completing the real work.

Once a routine meeting or progress report is established, clearly define roles and responsibilities. This will hold people, including you, accountable to meeting the deadlines and keeping people informed of status updates. Knowing who is doing what and when is a critical component of time management.

When dealing in team situations, it's also important to divide and conquer. Not everyone needs to be at every meeting. Have someone who attended the meeting provide an update and any key deliverables to the collective group. Also, it's important for you to schedule actual *work* time for yourself and/or sub-group to ensure time is not all spent in meetings relating to what is being asked of you. As for meetings taking up all of your day, you have the right and obligation, whether you are the organizer or not, to question when meetings have run their course and are no longer valuable. Don't have meetings to set up meetings. Look to get rid of time-wasting tasks.

Understand the importance of working as a team. A group of people can get more done in less time than one person if the process and roles are managed well. It is obvious, but is not always done effectively.

ASSESSING YOUR CHECKLIST HABITS

I used to work with an individual who carried her calendar with her everywhere. Within the calendar was her personal checklist for the day. Each morning, I would see her flipping the pages back and forth from yesterday to today and transferring the items not finished yesterday to the new day. After several days of watching her do this, I finally asked her two questions: First, how long does it take each day to transfer the new items over? Second, how important were the tasks in the first place if they kept getting moved? The answers were, that it took longer than she liked and the tasks transferred each day were probably not as important as she had originally thought. She was hurting her ability to manage time effectively in an attempt to organize each day.

The use of checklists always starts with the best intentions. Unfortunately, people often like to see them to *check* off their completed items and turn it into an accomplishments list. Checklists shouldn't be used as an accomplishments list to tick off the little victories, or as an exercise in procrastination. Checklists should be used to drive execution of the tasks, but too often we start to migrate to the easier and quicker tasks. If you want an accomplishments list, then keep one, but don't combine it with your checklist. A checklist should be about getting things done. On it should be all items needing to be addressed today: important, not important, urgent, and not urgent. It should be a complete list dedicated to today.

Assess your own checklist usage. Whether it is a literal checklist or a figurative set of tasks that you keep online, take the time to understand how often you move tasks regularly. You should stop using a checklist if you constantly shift tasks from day to day—this isn't productive. Consider the following when conducting your assessment, some of which is reinforcement of past chapters:

- If you have moved a task for consecutive days, you must ask yourself, "How important is it?" If it is important, take action on it. If it is important but not urgent, don't schedule it for tomorrow, schedule it for a week from now, when you know you can get to it.

- If you are proactively staying ahead of your day, week, and month as stated in an earlier chapter, then you should be on top of this and simply be making tweaks along the way.

- Checklists, if kept, must be comprised of the least amount of work you expect to get done and still consider the day a success. Specifically, this is the "I can't leave until this gets done" list. Be very realistic.

- Build in daily events and habits. What do you do at eight a.m. every morning? Are there calls you have to return, administrative tasks that need to be done (e.g., paperwork to process)? If so, build it in. Account for the time you are using.

When it comes to checklists, the important key is to not write it down or add it to your online to-do list today if you are not going to do it today. Your checklist assessment should enable you to turn a potential time management hindrance into a time management tool.

CREATING EFFECTIVE CHECKLISTS

In an ironic twist on the previous chapter, I want to share the power of mindless checklists. As I was packing for a summer vacation, I was scrambling around and getting stressed over whether or not I was forgetting something. As I was digging through my junk drawer, in the back of a notebook I found last year's list. There it was; everything I needed to bring—including a swimsuit, sunscreen, and sunglasses. The burdensome task of packing turned from a budding stressful situation to a quick to-do. I have since made a winter vacation list, and a business trip list. Each of the lists has matured and changed over time, but the basics remain the same. Routines—or doing the same thing over again with predictability—can make you a better organizer and time manager if they enhance your productivity and reduce your stress levels.

Determine what checklists and routines personally and professionally can work for you. Are there standard operating procedures that need to be made up? Are there morning opening or closing tasks that can be made holistic and easier for you to follow? What regular reference points or routines can you establish and create both personally and professionally? You might even want to establish a routine to have time each week, or even daily, for no electronic disruptions so that you can commit to doing nothing but what is in front of you. To put the last two chapters to work, you can have an appointment for today to review the specific checklist that will be used (e.g., "Use packing list to pack for vacation").

Checklists and routines reduce unpredictability and consistently let everyone know ahead of time what is expected. If it's a standing meeting or a common task that makes you more productive and reduces unnecessary stress, then checklists and routines can and should be implemented.

MONITORING MULTITASKING

I have been involved in many meetings, especially conference calls, in which people were obviously not engaged. The disengaged population is often multitasking. Besides the people who readily admit that they are multitasking (you would be surprised at the number of people who come right out and tell me), there are the people who don't say a word during the entire meeting, other than to say hello in the beginning and goodbye at the end. The multitaskers also are the obvious ones who say, "Huh?" or, "Can you please repeat the question?" when they hear their name directly. Some are bold enough to say, "Johnny and I were just instant messaging and I didn't catch all that."

In 2009, Ryan Buxton referenced a new study from the Proceedings of the National Academy of Sciences that found multitasking may do more harm than good. Citing the study's findings, the article states, "Multitaskers are more susceptible to memory interference by irrelevant details." The effort to move from one topic to another and the exertion required to return where you were impacts the true retention of information for multitaskers. What does this have to do with time management? Everything. Anything that takes your concentration away from the present will create extra work for you. Stop kidding yourself by thinking that multitasking saves time. It actually does the opposite.

I recently saw a presenter request the audience to write out their first name and last name. He asked them to write out the first letter of their first name followed by the first letter of their last name, and so on. It obviously took much longer than simply writing their names out normally. The point was powerful.

Start an exercise over the next three days at work. I want it to be based on true experiential facts, not by looking at the past and creating a time study—you want facts, not subjectivity. Start to monitor the number of times that you try to multitask in a day. By being conscientious of it, you will reduce the pull to do it. Mark down the number of attempts, even if you went back to concentrating on the first item. The goal is to improve this by ten percent each day.

I won't be a hypocrite and say that I have never done it. However, since I've limited my multitasking, I have found myself asking *What just happened?* in a meeting much less frequently than I had in the past. Additionally, I will say that my concentration level and my engagement has grown substantially since I made a concerted effort to concentrate on one task, one meeting, and one conversation at a time. A conversation that only needs to happen once—thus saving everyone time.

COMMITTING YOURSELF

Have you ever been on a conference call and waited several minutes after the start time of the meeting to actually begin? What if each time a person joins late, the host stops and provides a catch-up summary? Is that fair to people who joined on time? How about meetings that extend beyond the scheduled end time with no regard for what anyone else may have scheduled next? I've been in all of the above, in each of these roles: on time, late, host, and guest. As the host, I finally made a commitment to start the meeting on time and end on time. Commitment is a critical skill in time management. I realized I needed to be more committed with several factors of my time management. By committing myself to building better habits, I found that others started to practice similar techniques.

Understand your own commitment level. Be fully invested in improving your time management skills, and be respectful of others' time, as well. Think of examples in which you must commit and start to create the right actions and habits. Here are some examples:

- Commit to start and end times you set for yourself. If you said you would spend an hour on a project, stick to that time. If you're not done with a task, set up a new time to complete it.

- The same holds true as the host of a meeting. Start on time and end on time. In a meeting, you may want to say, "Out of respect for everyone's time, we're going to get started." It's not always easy, but many times we enable the process. With every new late attendee who joins, we do a quick recap. As much as we want everyone on the same page, it makes the meeting inefficient and is disrespectful to those who did join on time. You can offer to catch them up after the call or have them read the meeting minutes, but it's important to try to limit the constant recaps for the late arrivers.

- As the end of a meeting approaches, you may want to say, "I see we only have a few minutes remaining. We'll end the meeting and cover the rest at the next meeting," or set up a new time to finish that works for everyone. Going beyond the end time has a downstream effect for many. Showing respect for other people's calendars builds the right habits for everyone. Be committed to making it happen.

Stay focused on doing what you set out to do, starting by sticking to what you allotted for time on your calendar. This will keep you on task, build a strong time management reputation for you, and ultimately save time for not only yourself, but others. Looking back at incidents when you let time drift or found yourself not committing to what you set out to do will provide you with a good snapshot of what needs to change and what new habits to establish.

TAKING TIME TO ASSESS STRATEGIES

There was a peer of mine whom I would often call and have to leave messages. She would never return my calls. As soon as I sent her an instant message, she was prompt with her communication and we were always able to get things done. By tailoring our communication styles to her preferences, we were both more efficient. Who you're communicating with, what you're communicating, and how you're communicating it will positively or negatively impact your time. Confidence, influencing others, persuasion skills, setting clear expectations, being clear and concise—all are tied to effective communication and time management. All are a must when it comes to being productive, not to mention building stronger relationships.

If you sit in meetings that have consistently been a waste of time, are you confident enough to offer solutions to make them more effective, or strong enough to say they should be held less frequently, or even stopped altogether? Whether it is speaking up during the meeting or after it to let the host know, communication does drive time management.

How effective are your listening skills? Are you truly paying attention and listening to people? Think back to the number of times when questions had to unnecessarily be addressed again because one person wasn't listening? Listening is another key component of communication and, again, time management.

I can't state it enough: communication is an extremely important facet of effective time management. Assess your communication strategies, then go out and commit to and share best practices around communication and time management. Take time to:

- Understand communication preferences for those you work with the most. If you don't know, then ask.

- Use the right channel based on priority. Is an email and instant message (IM) the right channel based on the urgency or expected actions? Don't send an email to deal with fire drills needing immediate attention—you can't expect everyone to be on email at all times of the day. You might send an instant message to get someone's attention, but you want to avoid ping-ponging the message back and forth when details can be discussed quickly on the phone.

- Be conscientious of the audience when sending emails. Give summaries and highpoints, if necessary, and details to only those who really need them. It saves you time in writing and other people's time in reading. Also, be concise by not writing the email version of *War and Peace* to ask a simple question.

- Know who needs and wants to know. Don't reply to everyone on the email distribution (*reply all*) unless it is truly needed and impacts *all*—it cuts down on potential unnecessary email return responses.

Communication plays an important role when establishing priorities and making all of us conscientious about being productive and not wasting time. Looking at how you've chosen to communicate in the past and establishing new reliable strategies will enhance your efficiency.

MANAGING YOUR EMAIL

According to bizcommunity.com, it was estimated that 294 billion emails are sent each day, with about seventy-five percent considered spam, per estimates by the Radicati Group (2010). Getting through the seventy-five percent, plus the twenty-five percent you need for actual work, takes up valuable time. Now, imagine that every time you receive a new message, a bell sounds or a preview notice of incoming mail comes into view. When that happens, it grabs your attention and starts to pull you toward multitasking. We live in a very reactive work environment now. Sending and receiving emails has made us slaves to this form of communication, and keeps us leashed to whatever device gets us that information. Take back control and be proactive in dealing with ancillary email impacts. Let's start to implement concrete email strategies.

- Block off and dedicate time to manage your email. Whether you do it in the morning, before lunch, late afternoon, or all of the above, you should have dedicated time for it and not take them on one at a time, throughout the day.

- Ignore new messages. Rather than behaving like Pavlov's dog and responding to every bell that rings telling you that "You have mail," become proactive and take control of when you choose to spend time reading email.

- Deal with it one time. Remember to touch an email once. Take action on the emails such as moving it to another location or scheduling a meeting or a phone call, but don't read it and keep it there. This causes you to read it multiple times.

- Resist the immediate temptation to grab your smart phone. Don't read emails immediately when you wake up. This will create an instant heavy workload and frustrated state of mind. Give yourself a chance to adjust to your day prior to checking your email.

- Turn off the feature that confirms you have a new email or provides a preview; you don't want the distraction of knowing that an email came in. If you're blocking off time and have set expectations with those you work with, you don't need these features.

- Avoid unnecessary 'thank you' emails. They often create an avalanche of somewhat meaningless emails that go back and forth. If it is truly worthy, call or write a heartfelt note. In my first six months at a new job, I had over thirteen hundred emails saying some version of thank you. There were some that were heartfelt, but there were others that were less sincere and simply read "thx." The emails caught my attention and forced me to stop what I was doing to delete them.

- Simplify your organization. I recommend against setting up auto-filtering to organize emails by categories, senders, etc. It creates the need to look in multiple places when researching or looking for something. You should do your organizing through file management, since you get information from many sources, not just email. Build strong online file management systems to assist in searching for pertinent material.

Taking a proactive, methodical, and strategic approach to email management will allow you to take back your day and become a more productive professional.

SETTING THE ALARM

I set an alarm to wake up in the morning, but it rarely goes off since my internal clock always wakes me up about fifteen minutes before the scheduled time. On the few days it does beep in my ear, my day usually doesn't start out calmly because I've learned to rely on the extra fifteen minutes. I become rushed and stressed, and find that this mentality carries over into the rest of the day.

I've watched colleagues rush through the door late for work while carrying a bag of donuts or a cup of coffee. Although I understand that breakfast is considered the most important meal of the day, I personally wondered about the decision to make the extra stop if they knew they were close to their start time and would most likely be late. But let's not harp on that. The important thing to focus on is that this rushed and harried feeling sets the tone for each of us, and influences how clearly we think, how productive we are, and yes, our organizational skills for the rest of the day.

As king of the obvious, I want you to get up earlier—base the new time on how it fits in your schedule, but buy at least fifteen minutes of fluff time. If it means going to bed earlier, then work that piece into your overall schedule as well. Give yourself some breathing room before your shift or day starts so that you aren't rushed. Try to set a calming tone to your day. For those individuals who like to play games with themselves by setting a clock or watch earlier or later, I recommend against it. Besides the fact that you're no longer synchronized with the rest of the people in your time zone, you're actually self-initiating stress as you are constantly converting to the real time.

It's important to start our day right with an easy wake-up and plenty of time to get ready. Our starting attitudes and productivity as we calmly walk through the door with plenty of time to spare will send positive messages to your brain that you intend to handle the day in a fully capable manner!

BLENDING WORK AND LIFE SCHEDULES

I used to work through lunch. By the end of the day, I'd be worn out, but I needed that hour to get through all the work that I had ahead of me… Or did I? Remaining committed to our goals—whether it means walking away from the desk or following through to handle a customer's request—continues to build our reputation and credibility, and thus impacts our success relative to our organization and time management. I started to commit to reserving my lunch time for non-work activity. The actual time may vary each day, but I make sure that I get away.

I typically like to go for a run to clear my head, but the message here is to commit to doing what you want to do. I find that when I come back to the desk, I have a fresh perspective and new energy to drive through the rest of the day productively. Running is just one example of keeping a clear head by balancing my personal and professional needs. The key is to move your focus away from work, even for a short period of time, and to bring back a laser-focused approach upon your return. Today's professional environment and all the technology therein mean that work and life are interlaced. As much as we want to separate the two, it's almost impossible. So instead of fighting it, it's time to embrace it.

You can start by blending your personal and professional schedules together. If it's not permitted at work, then at least counterbalance them, and view them side by side to ensure that you are looking at both worlds together. Your commitment to balancing work and life will bring more control to both. Schedule your lunches, or they will never happen. Block off time for dentist appointments or they will be forgotten. Include time on your calendar needed to pick up your children from school or let the dog out so that you won't schedule one event to inadvertently create a conflict with the other.

BEING CURIOUS

When a colleague of mine initially started publishing a required report each day, he would get regular questions about it. As time passed, the number of questions subsided. He figured the report had run its course, but he was asked to keep producing it for no reason except that it had always been done that way. He cleverly added a box on the report that read, "Space for Rent." Over a year, not one person questioned it or even commented on it. He changed the frequency of sending the report to weekly before eventually stopping—and no one questioned it.

Don't accept that "It's always been that way." Let's take a trip back to our childhood. Why is the sky blue? Where do babies come from? Okay, let's keep the last one out of it. The point is to get back to the natural childhood curiosity that many of us grew out of. As important as routines are for us to maintain stability in our day, when was the last time you brought your natural curiosity to work? Routines are only as good as our ability to understand their value.

Why is this report important to read each day? What am I gaining by attending this meeting if my peer is already there and can report back? Why am I working late? Is it because real work needs to be done, or is it because I'm trying to impress someone? The answers to these real questions can serve to help you find pockets of wasted time. There may be opportunities for collaboration, teamwork, or even just stopping a practice that is no longer effective.

It's time to be a curious child again. Starting today, question the whys to what you're doing. Why do I need to travel to some meetings when I can be just as productive over the phone? Why have I allowed junk mail to clutter my inbox as opposed to unsubscribing? There are many questions that can and should be asked. You may find that the answers confirm that a particular task does indeed add value to the work you're doing. That's a good thing. Keep doing that task. What you're looking for are the pockets of unproductive time that you can eliminate. You might surprise yourself and your co-workers with more time to concentrate on the more important tasks.

UNDERSTANDING PRIORITIES

Each morning a peer of mine would settle into her desk, log in to her system, then walk down to the café, chat with friends, and slowly make her way back to the office to start her day. She had the flexibility to do this after her eight a.m. start time, so I'm not making judgments on how she started her day. The judgment comes into play when she would complain—almost daily—that she didn't have time to do anything, insisting that her "plate was full." All of our plates are full. The question is, what bite do we need to take first to clear it? If her top priority is to get coffee, she has made a decision that this is more important, and in some cases, more urgent than other matters. Each day is full of decisions and judgments. Each one has repercussions and downstream effects. When we better understand the differences between urgent versus non-urgent and important versus not important, we start to make better decisions.

A boss may say, "I need you to do something right away." Is it important and is it urgent? You may still have to assess and ask questions such as the due date, competing priorities, and similar requests made in the past.

You may have two very urgent and important items, yet one will always outweigh the other. Make assessments; ask questions. In our assessment, we need to ask real or rhetorical questions until we're prepared to make a decision about which one comes first. Another aspect to consider and respect is that what might be urgent and/or important to you may not be important and/or urgent to others. Frequently, we make assumptions based on our own feelings and interpretations. Make no assumptions.

I want you to draw a square with four boxes inside. In each square, I want you to write *urgent, not urgent, important,* and *not important* in separate boxes. Then, take your schedule for the next week and start to plot out the expected work. Label them based on where they fall on this matrix. This will help you determine where to spend your time. The outcome doesn't dictate that every urgent and important item takes precedent over non-urgent tasks all of the time. It simply lets you decide which items to tackle first and what items to reserve for later. We often take the opposite tack by gravitating toward the easiest tasks because they give us a sense of accomplishment. But in order to be successful at managing time, it's critical to learn how to best combine the important and the easier tasks.

ACCOUNTING FOR PERSONAL CONVERSATIONS

I used to work with a friend who had the same schedule, so we always walked out together each day. But, I found that his end time of five o'clock p.m. and my end time of five p.m. weren't the same. The clocks read the same, and we would often start packing up for the evening at the same time, but we were never ready at the same time. Sure, a customer might call, or colleagues needed our attention at the moment we'd planned on originally leaving. This is understood; it happens sometimes. However, what I found was that it happened to him consistently.

He was a social butterfly. He would go from person to person and spend what seemed like hours talking away about nothing important. As someone who teaches networking and the importance of relationships, I get it. However, there is a balancing act. He often complained that there just weren't enough hours in the day to do everything he wanted, personally and professionally. There are enough hours—the question is, where do you want to spend them? Once I made him conscious of my observation of his nonproductive wanderings, he assessed himself and readjusted accordingly. His hallway conversations still met the needs of building relationships. His conversations didn't have to be terse, but he found a nice balance and actually was recognized for his productivity a few months later.

Assess how much of your day is spent on random personal conversation, and determine if it is negatively impacting your ability to get things done. This does not mean you can't be *personal*. It simply means, don't spend forty-five minutes talking about the weekend and then complain that you don't have enough time in the day to do your tasks. It might mean a five-minute chat and a genuine, "Great to see you" before you move on. What's more important at work: relationship building *or* time management? If you find the right balance, this becomes an *and* statement, not an *or*, enabling you to navigate through the important social *and* professional aspects of your job.

CREATING OUR OWN PRESSURES

I was juggling quite a few projects at one time. I was balancing important and not important, urgent and not urgent, I was putting in the hours and efforts, and still one of my projects went beyond the deadline. Yet, it passed without a word from my boss, or anyone else for that matter. As much as I try to do everything I can to communicate progress to the powers that be, in this case, it slipped through the cracks and I didn't provide any heads-up. For the record, as previously stated, I will emphasize that communication is critical in these matters. Somehow, in this case it wasn't done. I had what I thought were the right priorities—a strong relationship with my boss and no intentions of hiding anything—so I let him know that the deadline had passed, and told him my plans for completion. His response?

"Oh yeah, I forgot about that. Get it to me when you can. No hurry."

Let's go back to the comment that communication is critical to time management. When originally told about the initiative, I should have asked the following question: "What happens if the deadline is missed?" I should have ensured that *our* priorities were the same. We sometimes have our own internal pressures that are far greater than reality. Do you put more pressure on yourself than anyone else? Reign in some of the pressure and give yourself a break.

It's time to add the appropriate questions to your arsenal when asked to complete a project. Start by asking when the deadline is, and follow it up with a version of the question, "What happens if the deadline isn't met?"

Getting an idea of the true urgency is important in order to match priorities with the requestor. If he or she says you'll be fired if you don't meet the deadline, then I think you understand the priorities. But in all seriousness, if you form the habit of asking questions about prioritization and urgency from the actual requester, you'll build trust with your colleagues and supervisors and ensure that everyone is consistently attuned to the same goals.

TAKING NOTES

I had only been in the real world working for about six months. I was doing decently on the phones, and was promoted to a job with more responsibilities. I was still on the phones, but we had more meetings to discuss strategies. I showed up to my first meeting without a notebook, paper, or any other way to retain the information. My boss called me out on it; I have never gone to a meeting again without something to keep notes.

According to culturalorientation.net, retention rates for adult learning varies based on the teaching method, but dips as low as five percent for lectures. Individuals learn best when they are actively engaged and taking notes. Culturalorientation.net noted in their article that, "As Confucius said nearly twenty-five hundred years ago, 'I hear and I forget. I see and I remember.'"

Since that day, I've been a consummate note taker. What does this have to do with organization and time management? It has to do with follow-up, prioritization, and execution; adding everything to your calendar and ensuring that you're actually doing what was discussed right the first time!

If you have not consistently brought something to take notes with during meetings, start immediately. Always take a notebook to meetings, and actually use it. The value isn't the notes staring blankly back at you. The significance comes into play when you invest the time to go back and read them—and take action. Just as you would when taking action on emails, it's important to do the same with notes. Go back and refer to them to determine whether any actions need to be taken. Do you have questions that still need to be asked, or is clarification or confirmation still needed? Do you know if you were specifically asked to do something? If yes, mark it accordingly, and immediately add it to your calendar to get it done. I use markings for items that require immediate action to ensure that they stand out. Then, I immediately begin the transfer from paper or even tablet to calendar. For those who prefer note taking directly online, you're even further ahead. I prefer actual written notes because I've found that the writing and transferring of information has helped my retention rates significantly, but use what works best for you. What is important is that you don't simply take notes and then ignore them—that would be a waste of time.

PUTTING OFF TASKS

I used to have a person work for me who managed a small group of employees. She was great with people, but lacked effective organization skills. We had been working on these skills, and I had seen some improvement. I then sat down at her desk one day and looked behind her. Her credenza had been left open, and obviously was not intended for me to see.

She was a file hoarder. She had mountains of unfiled paperwork, personnel files, and who knows what else, hidden in the pile. She said she would get around to it. So, we set a deadline. I came back the day after the deadline had passed; her credenza looked very much the same. She said she'd tried, but it was too much and she didn't have time. As stated throughout this book, we do have time; it's just a matter of what we do with it. The simplicity of putting the files behind her to get to them later turned into a pressure-filled ticking time bomb that still had to be addressed versus a series of quick actions. The mess was a big concern. Think about the fact that personal information in the files was accessible, potential follow-up items were left unattended, and that there were possible audit issues depending on what was in the pile.

She saw a stack of work that became psychologically difficult to attack. Her strategy was *avoidance*. I've rarely seen this strategy work. I saw a series of immediate and small tasks that could be completed quickly, enabling her to gain efficiency in the future. We tackled it together—in less than thirty minutes. In daily life, we often put off things that appear to be burdensome tasks, which can take away from our attention to detail and may even cause our stress to increase. Try shifting your mindset, so that you approach tasks as they come up with the same urgency you associate with tasks after you've let them build.

If you have always filed and saved immediately, you're on the right path. If you don't, then today is the day to start.

When something needs to be filed, do it immediately—or, depending on your position, delegate it immediately—whether it is a paper, email content, or anything online that needs to be saved, recorded, and/or filed. In order to maximize your efficiency, it's important that you know where things are at all times. Knowing that it's under the third pile to the left may work sometimes, but this is about consistency. How you file and where you choose to put things is up to you. The goal is to have an organized methodology.

MAKING DECISIONS

I used to work in a credit acquisition department where we were making lending decisions for customers every day. The customer would send in an application, and we had to make a credit decision based on multiple factors like previous credit and financial history. Every effort was made to build consistency, but there were always situations when we would be on the fence due to the subjective nature of the job. Do we approve it, decline it, or ask for more information from the customer? The easy decision was to ask for more information, but even then, some information that came back still left us in the fog. Our job was to make sound decisions that didn't put the bank at risk, but we still had regulations and certain internal deadlines that forced us to make some kind of determination. We called these final decisions endlines. We had to endline and stop waffling. Right or wrong, we had to make an educated and informed decision before the application was considered past due.

In your professional life, it's important to realize that procrastination is not an option. There are decisions that have to be made. Effective today, you will learn to make *endline* decisions. You obviously want to gather important facts to make important decisions. However, there are some decisions that aren't important. Certain emails may be sitting in your inbox that you've read twenty-five times in the hope that something can be done to deal with it. Have you engaged the right people, have you escalated the situation, have you gathered the right facts? In the touch-it-once mentality, leaving it in your inbox doesn't solve the problem. A decision still needs to be made. Being decisive and attacking problems head-on will always save you time and effort. If you're in the habit of leaving items unattended because you find it difficult deciding what to do, now is the time to commit to changing that habit. An unofficial rule of thumb for me is to consider a maximum of five business days before simply making an *endline* decision—give or take, based on the circumstances. Even if you choose to delete it with no actions, you still have to make a decision. It's been a week already! As long as you understand the ramifications of your decisions, you will start to build the right habits and reduce the volume of these endline decisions significantly.

ASKING FOR HELP

I received a panicked phone call from a colleague one day who said she had taken on additional responsibilities and that she felt she was drowning, her nose barely above water. She was crumbling under the weight of her responsibilities. After she'd calmed down, she asked the simplest question of all: "Can you help me?" Whether she called me or someone else, she had become self-aware enough to know her work performance was suffering. Self-awareness is a powerful tool.

Too many people wait until it's too late to ask for assistance. You don't need to complain, you need to look for solutions. If you find that these solutions or other time management tools you've tried aren't working for you—keep searching. Telling someone it will get done still doesn't get it done, until you find the time to do it. If you're falling behind, be strong enough to get assistance. You don't want to wait for a time study to figure out what you do all day! If you don't know, ask a peer, ask a boss, ask a mentor, even ask a stranger, but make sure that you ask. I realize we're in a do-more-with-less business world. We hesitate to talk with people about the time crunches we're under. We don't want to be considered weak, inefficient, unproductive, or other negative connotations that can hurt our professional growth. Work not getting done, however, will be a much bigger problem over time.

It's time to do some soul searching. Is today the day to ask for help with your own organization and time management skills? Even if you want more time to implement these strategies, set an actual deadline to do another assessment. If you reach that date and are not at the level you expected, make that the day to ask for help. As stated in an earlier chapter, the concept of building a strong enough relationship with someone to have this type of conversation is critical. Invest the time now to build strong relationships with those people around you who can help. Discuss challenges with your manager and other co-workers, and even people you mentor with to get sound advice. Silence will only hurt you. Communicate with your manager and the appropriate people within your organization relating to what's on your plate. It may take time to reach a solution, but it always begins with self-awareness.

CREATING TIME FOR YOU

As an immature manager who hadn't realized how important the people working for him were, I would come home every night saying that I should be paid extra for babysitting. I even moved my computer from the front of my desk to the back corner in an attempt to reduce the volume of questions. It didn't help, but I did quickly gain a reputation for being unapproachable (I will remind you that I wasn't ready to manage people). I was moved out of the role, but that's a story for another day—it does end well (see *The Transformation of a Doubting Thomas* for details).

Why was I so frustrated with people asking me questions to solve customer problems or wanting my attention in order to build a stronger employee-manager relationship? It took some soul searching, but I did figure it out. What I found was that I allowed one-hundred percent of my time to be swallowed up by others who were dependent on me, and I found myself not knowing when or how I would get everything else done. If you're a parent or even have pets, you may know the feeling that we sometimes just need a little time alone to do what we need for ourselves.

What I learned was that I simply had to create that time. It didn't have to be long periods. Whether it was a quick five-minute breather or going to a quiet office to write a performance appraisal, that time made me concentrate on the task at hand. As a result, I became more productive and could then give one-hundred percent concentration when I returned. The built-up frustration of wanting to do something only to encounter obstacles because of the pull from those depending on us hurts our relationship building, and our time management.

When it makes sense, put up your own "Do Not Disturb" sign when you absolutely have to get work done. This can be literal or figurative, done with an online indicator for instant messaging, for example, or by walking away from your desk. Either way, proactively let people know that you're temporarily not available. If you're on vacation, turn on your out-of-office message. You can also practice just letting your phone go to voicemail and allowing emails to come in without an immediate response. Next, turn off the distractions that can take away from your actual work. Don't sneak a peek at Facebook—your friends will still be there later.

You can be more productive and reduce frustration and interruptions by simply being obvious about your availability—people will respect it. Let people know that you're temporarily not available, but that when you return they will have your undivided attention.

TAKING BACK YOUR DAY

The concept of time is manmade, yet as the centuries passed, the lone town church bell that marked the end of another work day somehow became the need to manage every second of every day. As a result, we have blurred the lines between work and life. We have a choice every day in what to do with the twenty-four hours that are staring us in the face. I've been anal retentive and a consummate time management teacher—and student—for many years. Yet, I don't wear a watch. No, I don't use sun-dials, but we are surrounded by apparatus that tell us the time. It's on cell phones, computers, and even in my small New England church bell tower, which chimes every hour.

To me, time is the present, not a device. We can't live in the past, we are only in this very moment, and we can make the future better by managing our present effectively. Time management is all mental. It's about commitment, routine, flexibility, adjustment, and planning. I gave a person I mentor specific instructions to do something to develop herself. She agreed it was reasonable, and committed to doing it. She didn't do it. Her exact words were, "I didn't do it because I didn't have time." That's too bad. It doesn't hurt me, but it also doesn't develop her. I can't force her to do it, but she couldn't commit to finding herself thirty minutes a month for her own growth. We create our own self-limitations. We say we'll do tomorrow what we really want to do today.

It's time to take back your work day. Today is about self-reflection in order to understand what else you need to control your work day. This comes from understanding what's holding you back, thinking it through, having the right conversations, and taking action to improve.

Time management is a requirement for all levels in an organization. If you think you don't have enough time to invest in improving your own time management, think again. There are only twenty-four hours in the day. They should not all be devoted to work, but if you don't manage the work piece, you can't balance the personal piece. Start immediately.

In time management terms, that's now.

REFERENCES

"Adult Learning and Retention." Cultural Orientation Resource Center, September 13, 2012. http://www.culturalorientation.net/content/download/480/3397/file/Tools%20for%20Trainers%20Tools%20for%20Trainers%20Adult_Learning.pdf.

Anal-retentive." Memidex/WordNet Dictionary/Thesaurus. Accessed September 6, 2014. http://www.memidex.com/anal-retentive.

Beck, Dave. "Don't Let Technology Take Over." *San Antonio Express-News*, April 29, 2007. http://www.basex.com/press.nsf/InFrames/3A2BCA9F51B35D6E852572D90012FEE0.

Buxton, Ryan. "Study: Multitasking may be detrimental to information retention." *LSU Reveille*, September 7, 2009. http://www.lsureveille.com/news/study-multitasking-may-be-detrimental-to-information-retention/.

Carlson, Richard, *Don't Sweat the Small Stuff…and it's all small stuff.* New York: Hyperion, 1997.

EVERLYTIC Press Release. "Return Path partnership good news for pMailer clients." Bizcommunity.com, November 30, 2011. http://www.bizcommunity.com/Article/196/16/67930.html.

Frank, Adam, *About Time: Cosmology and Culture at the Twilight of the Big Bang.* New York: Free Press, 2011.

ACKNOWLEDGEMENTS

I want to thank my wife, Ellen, and three daughters Meg, Erin, and Tatum for their unwavering support of my writing, speaking, radio hosting, and every other crazy idea that has popped into my head. I wouldn't be able to do any of it well without effectively managing my time. More importantly, none of it can be done without the people most important in my life. I love each of you deeply.

I'm also so appreciative of my editor, Jen Blood, who has left her fingerprints on every book that I've written. She not only provides valuable insight to the content and grammar, she thinks strategically to ensure the reader is influenced, thinks differently, and is changed by the words. Whether it is the importance of an impactful subtitle or asking if what is written is my best, I know my book isn't ready until she has seen it. I also can't forget my consistent first-draft editor, Beth Chamberlin, who will someday get the difference between *then* and *than* into my thick head.

When it comes to time management, I want to thank the first boss I had when managing people for the first time, for forcing me to go to a training session on time management. I had no thoughts—positive or negative—about the course. Yet, I came back with an understanding of how important it was to manage my professional time well. I didn't realize it, but on my professional rollercoaster ride of ups and downs, none of the downs could ever be blamed on not getting work done. I refused to allow *not having enough time* to become an easy excuse for me to falter, or an easy reason for my management team to say I wasn't cutting it. By managing my time well, I was able to concentrate on the real business of relationship building, leadership, and learning from my mistakes.

I want to thank the people who said "F-U"—you know who you are, because you know that *follow-up* became a critical tool in my arsenal. When I was new to numerous positions and roles over the past twenty-five years, even when I didn't know what I was doing, people still had confidence that an answer was coming—even if I didn't have that answer, yet. Each of you has taught me the powerful relationship between time management and people.

I want to thank my coaching clients and people who continue to spread the word about my organization and time management skills. You have given me the confidence to push my time management—and training—skills further.

To go back to my early childhood *Sesame Street* viewing, I want to thank the word "No." Time management is about knowing who and what to say *no* to, where and when to say it, and, most importantly, how to say *no*. When managed appropriately, the word *yes* can be used more often. You can do everything you want to do if you prioritize and execute correctly.

ALSO BY THOMAS B. DOWD III

The Transformation of a Doubting Thomas: Growing from a Cynic to a Professional in the Corporate World

ISBN: 978-1-938883-06-4

2012 Honorable Mention New England Book Festival in the "Business" category

During his inconsistent first twenty years in a business environment, author Thomas Dowd learned lessons, both positive and negative, which transformed into shared professional success. Those experiences empower readers to differentiate themselves and work smarter—not harder—to thrive in a chaotic corporate culture that, due to current economic conditions, encourages the employed and unemployed alike to simply try to survive.

Available for purchase at www.transformationtom.com and online booksellers everywhere.

Available in print and eBook formats.

ALSO BY THOMAS B. DOWD III

From Fear to Success: A Practical Public-speaking Guide

ISBN: 978-1-938883-04-0

2013 Axiom Business Book Awards Gold Medal in the "Business Reference" category

2013 Honorable Mention Paris Book Festival and New York Book Festivals in the "How-to" and "Business" categories, respectively

Dizzy head. Pounding heart. Shaking limbs. Sweating body. Shallow breathing. Queasy stomach. These symptoms hold people back from what they really want: SUCCESS. An easy-to-read guide to overcome anxiety and relate to any audience, *From Fear to Success* will resonate with public speakers at all levels on their journey to communication confidence.

Available for purchase at www.transformationtom.com and online booksellers everywhere.

Available in print, eBook, and audiobook formats.

ALSO BY THOMAS B. DOWD III

Displacement Day: When My Job was Looking for a Job

ISBN: 978-1-62865-078-5

2014 Honorable Mention Paris Book Festival and New York Book Festivals in the "General Non-Fiction" categories

On what was thought to be a typical work day, author Thomas Dowd received The Call Nobody Wants: "We're downsizing." In the midst of an economic downturn, the author had some choices to make in how to most effectively approach the new journey. *Displacement Day* is for anyone who has ever had the unfortunate—or fortunate—task of finding a job. Fortunate? Yes, because you may actually learn something about your character and resolve during the process that will change the course of your life and career. This book is a pick-me-up, motivational reference guide with clearly laid out objectives that give you the tools you need to successfully find a new professional occupation. More importantly, it lets you know that you're not alone in the process.

Available for purchase at www.transformationtom.com and online booksellers everywhere.

Available in print and eBook formats.

ABOUT THE AUTHOR

Tom Dowd is a graduate of the University of Delaware with a Communication degree concentrating on interpersonal and organizational communication. Tom is a prize-winning speaker, an award-winning author, trainer, and coach—all spurred by his need to be more than a painfully shy and introverted individual on a rollercoaster ride of success. As a member of Toastmasters International, he was awarded the District 45 Outstanding Toastmaster of the Year in 2011, representing over one-hundred clubs in Maine, New Hampshire, Vermont, and the three easternmost provinces of Canada. Tom is also a two-time impromptu District 45 Speech champion, and a member of the National Speakers Association and Global Speakers Federation.

Tom has over twenty-five years of experience in the financial industry in management, service, and leadership roles. He found success when he identified the correlation between building relationships, confidence in communication, routines, and time management. Tom has been teaching a similar version of the contents in this book for over fifteen years. In 2011, he started his own business, Thomas Dowd Professional Development & Coaching, LLC. There, he continues to use the lessons learned on his climb up the corporate ladder to help people creatively find ways to differentiate themselves in the workplace and find their own individual paths toward success. The mantra is, "Transform into who you really want to be." Transformation comes to those who *can get it all done.*

Tom lives in Camden, Maine with his wife and three daughters.

www.ingramcontent.com/pod-product-compliance
Lightning Source LLC
Chambersburg PA
CBHW071754170526
45167CB00003B/1019